CUBA

From Columbus to Castro

CUBA

From Columbus to Castro

by
Margot Williams & Josephine McSweeney

illustrated with photographs

Julian Messner ⓜ New York

JULIAN MESSNER and colophon are trademarks of Simon & Schuster, registered in the U.S. Patent and Trademark Office.

Manufactured in the United States of America.
Design by A Good Thing, Inc.

Guardian Newsweekly, pp. 34, 44-45, 50, 66-67
William Jaber, map p. 6
Library of Congress, p. 30
New York Public Library, p. 29
Queens Borough Public Library, pp. 25, 31
H. Armstrong Roberts, pp. 10 (top), 11
U.S. Coast Guard, pp. 37, 38
U.S. Navy, pp. 26, 28
Pictures not otherwise credited are by Josephine McSweeney.

Library of Congress Cataloging in Publication Data

Williams, Margot.
    Cuba from Columbus to Castro.

    Includes index.
    Summary: Traces the history of Cuba from its
discovery by Columbus to the present day and
discusses its economy, social structure, culture,
and government under the Castro regime.
        1. Cuba—History—Juvenile literature.
    2. Cuba—History—1959-   —Juvenile literature.
    [1. Cuba—History]   I. McSweeney, Josephine.
    II. Title.
    F1776.W54   972.91   81-16768
    ISBN 0-671-42501-3   AACR2

Contents

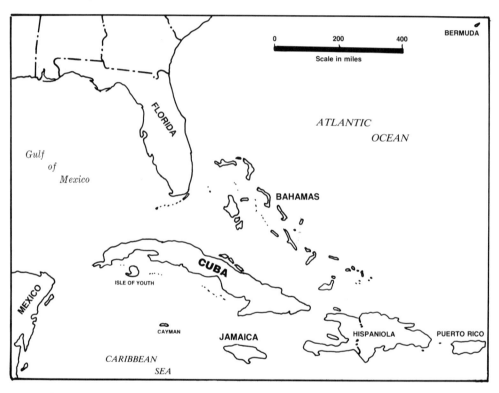

Cuba and her neighbors.

6

Arrival
in
Havana

An excited group of tourists from the United States await customs inspection in Havana's busy José Martí airport. Although the flight from Miami, Florida has taken only forty-five minutes, these tourists have covered a great symbolic distance. They are entering a country that has been closed to them for many years.

Before 1961, when diplomatic relations between the United States and Cuba were broken off, Havana was a favorite destination for vacationers. Beautiful beaches, luxurious hotels and restaurants, elegant gambling casinos made Cuba known as "America's Playland."

In 1959, a revolution led by Fidel Castro caused the overthrow of the government. When the new government took over large landholdings and industries owned by United States businesses, Washington stopped all trade and travel between the two nations for about sixteen years. But in 1977, President Jimmy Carter eased restrictions on travel. Once again, visitors from the United States were able to join the Canadians, Europeans, and Latin Americans who had continued to enjoy Cuba's warm climate and pleasant beaches.

In the airport among the many foreign travelers are visiting Cuban-Americans. Between 1959 and 1973 over 600,000 Cubans who disagreed with Castro's policies left or were forced to leave their homeland. Many settled in the United States. Now allowed to return as visitors, the Cuban-Americans bring suitcases filled with gifts for relatives. Most of the gifts are items unavailable in Cuba. Each item has to be reported to the customs inspector. The tourists fill in customs forms, change their American dollars for Cuban pesos, and are shown to their tour bus by a Cuban government guide. On the short ride to Havana city, the English-speaking guide begins to tell the tourists about Cuba's land and people.

Only ninety miles from Key West, Florida, the island of Cuba is the largest in the West Indies. It is 746 miles long —about the distance from New York to Chicago—and is 120 miles at its widest point. Cuba's territory also includes an offshore island, the Isle of Youth, formerly called the Isle of Pines, and about 1,600 small cays and islets. In area, Cuba is about the same size as Pennsylvania.

Because of its many excellent harbors and its strategic location between the Gulf of Mexico and the Caribbean Sea, Spanish explorers called Cuba the "Key to the New World." The United States and the Bahamas are to the north, Mexico is to the west, Jamaica and Hispaniola (the island made up of Haiti and the Dominican Republic) are to the south.

Although the island lies in the tropical zone, its climate is mild, with average temperatures of 77-80°F and plentiful rainfall. During the rainy season from May to November, hurricanes are likely to strike. Sometimes they cause great damage. In 1963 Hurricane Flora killed and injured thousands and destroyed crops and homes. Hurricane Allen severely damaged the grapefruit crop in 1980, but no lives were lost.

For the most part, Cuba's land is fertile. Flat or rolling plains suitable for farming and grazing lie between three mountain ranges. Although Cuba has 200 rivers, most are no larger than streams. However, they provide plentiful water for drinking and irrigation. This fortunate combination of climate and geography explains Cuba's agricultural success with crops like sugar cane, tobacco, and fruit. Cattle raising and fishing add to the food supply.

Cuba today reflects its Spanish, Indian, and African slave background. Blacks and **mulattoes,** those with black and Spanish parents, make up 62% of Cuba's population. **Mestizos,** of Indian and Spanish parents; **criollos,** whites born in Cuba; and **amarillos,** Chinese, make up the rest of the population of almost ten million.

Havana was founded in 1519 by the Spanish explorer Diego de Velásquez, and became Cuba's capital in 1589. Havana is Cuba's largest city and one of its fourteen provinces. A bustling government seat and commercial center, Havana is also filled with reminders of the Spanish colonial past. The entrance to the harbor is flanked by two castles built in the 1500s. Every night a chain was hung across the harbor between the castles to keep out foreign ships and pirates. Parts of a protective wall surrounding the old city are still visible. Pastel-colored houses line narrow streets which lead to lovely open squares.

Morro Castle protected Havana from pirates.

Part of Havana's old city wall.

The former capitol building, Havana.

Cuba's old capitol building was modeled on the United States Capitol in Washington, DC. Today it is a science center. Gracious houses which before Castro belonged to wealthy Cubans stand on streets lined with palm trees. They are now schools, dormitories, libraries and embassies.

The Presidential Palace of pre-revolutionary days has been turned into the Museum of the Revolution. There are many other museums in the Havana area, including "Finca Vigía," the home of the famous United States author, Ernest Hemingway. Landmarks from Hemingway's life and work are pointed out to tourists proudly.

Most tourists stay close to picturesque Havana and its Varadero beach, a ten mile stretch of fine white sand. Those

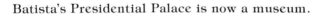

Batista's Presidential Palace is now a museum.

who take time to travel around the island can learn much more about the people, their history, and their way of life.

Tourists can visit the Isle of Youth which has been transformed by Cuban and foreign students into a showplace, with many new high schools in the countryside set among acres of grapefruit trees. Scuba divers and fishermen seek the varied and abundant sea life of its underwater coral reefs.

Traveling eastward from Havana province, buses made in Argentina and the Soviet Union pass seemingly endless fields of sugar cane, tobacco farms, and cattle ranches. In the midst of this fertile plain is the busy city of Santa Clara, with its textile mills, steel industry, and food processing plants. Another city, Cienfuegos, is noted for its ornate French-style architecture. Wide boulevards lead to a beautiful harbor filled with freighters from many countries. They have come to load up with sugar, for Cienfuegos has the largest sugar-shipping terminal in the world.

Still further eastward is the jewel of Sancti Spiritus province, Trinidad. Founded by the Spanish in 1514, Trinidad is a national treasure. Most of the streets are paved with cobblestones brought from New England as ship ballast. The buildings, in traditional Spanish style, are pastel stucco with red tile roofs. They have elaborate carved doors and tree-shaded arcades and courtyards. **Guarapo** stands dot the narrow streets, and thirsty passers-by stop for a cup of this cool, very sweet drink of sugar cane juice.

Traveling on, visitors see coffee and cocoa bushes covering the hillsides of mountainous Granma province in southeastern Cuba. In the fertile valley of the Cauto, Cuba's longest river, beans and other vegetables are raised near pastures of grazing cattle. Santiago de Cuba, the nation's second largest city, is built in the foothills of the Sierra Maestra mountains. Here are many sites famous in Cuba's struggle for independence from Spain and also in the Castro revolution.

Museum in Trinidad, Cuba.

Street in Cienfuegos, central Cuba.

Along the cross-country highway are many new housing developments. In Jibacoa, for example, there are four-story apartment buildings with balconies. In the center of the community is a school and a group of buildings which includes a bookstore, health station, day-care center, grocery, clothing store, and barber shop. There is also a large meeting room for the people of Jibacoa. This new community is part of a commune. Each family in the commune has given up the piece of land it once owned in exchange for a new rent-free apartment. The communal land is used for dairy farming. Family members work in the dairy cooperative that produces milk, cheese, and butter.

Jibacoa commune apartments.

The tourists' journey may end at the easternmost end of the island, at the port of Guantanamo, where the United States maintains a naval base. Six thousand United States citizens live and work on the forty-five square miles of the Guantanamo Bay Naval Base, separated from the rest of Cuba by a barbed wire fence.

Everywhere on the cross-country journey lines of schoolchildren can be seen on their way to work in the field. Militia members are glimpsed as they drill to defend Cuba against a feared United States invasion. Visitors from the United States may be surprised to see so many pre-1960 United States automobiles still in operation on Cuban streets. These cars—old Chevrolets, Pontiacs, Studebakers, and an occasional Edsel—were left behind by Americans and Cubans fleeing the revolution. Parts for the automobiles are unavailable in Cuba, so the owners repair

Most of the automobiles in Cuba are quite old.

these cars as best they can, because a new car is almost impossible to obtain. New cars made in Europe or the Soviet Union are used chiefly as taxis and for officials of the government.

And everywhere Cuban children are seen playing the national sport, baseball, which was brought to Cuba from the United States in earlier and friendlier times.

Tainos
to
Revolutionaries

When Christopher Columbus landed on Cuba's shores on October 27, 1492, he said it was "the loveliest land that human eyes have ever beheld." Friendly natives greeted him with gifts. Believing that he had reached the fabled wealth of the East Indies, Columbus called the natives "Indians."

Actually the natives were Tainos, an agricultural people who had gradually achieved dominance over an earlier cave-dwelling tribe, the Ciboneys. The Tainos gathered the fruit of the coconut, papaya, pineapple, and avocado trees and cultivated crops such as beans, potatoes, peanuts, maize (corn), and tobacco. Columbus was the first European to see how the tobacco leaf was rolled and smoked.

Christopher Columbus did not discover a new sea route to the riches of the Indies. Instead, he led the way to a "New World" beyond even his imagination. Following in his path came the Spanish **conquistadores** (conquerors). In 1511 Diego de Velásquez, a rich planter from the already conquered island of Hispaniola, landed at Baracoa with a military force in search of gold. The Taino natives had heard from Hispaniolan refugees about the harsh methods used by the Spanish **conquistadores**. A group of Tainos, led by their young chief, Hatuey, organized a war of resistance against the Spanish invaders. Although the Indians used guerrilla warfare methods of ambush and sneak attack, their primitive weapons could not defeat the enemy's guns and horses. Hatuey was captured and burned at the stake in 1512. He was the first hero in Cuba's long struggle for independence. And Diego de Velásquez became the first governor of Cuba.

As in the other colonies, Spanish priests followed the **conquistadores** to convert the Tainos to the Roman Catholic faith. The land was divided among the **conquistadores,** and natives were forced to work for them. Brutally treated and with no immunity to diseases brought by the Europeans, all but a few thousand Tainos were dead by the mid-1500s.

By 1515 there were already seven Spanish towns in the new colony, among them Havana. But the settlements grew slowly at first. The Spanish were busy exploring and

Christopher Columbus.

conquering the South American continent in expeditions led by Hernán Cortés and Francisco Pizarro. The port towns of Cuba were having their problems with pirates. They were supply points for ships returning to Spain laden with gold from the mines of Peru and Mexico—tempting targets for pirates. Buccaneers burned and looted Havana in 1538 and 1555. The Spanish built walls and forts to protect the city. Havana grew as more people moved to the safety of its fortifications.

Aside from port commerce, the main economic activity in the colony's early years was cattle raising. Agriculture did not achieve importance until Europeans developed a taste for tobacco. The King of Spain, realizing that large profits could be made on tobacco, maintained tight control on trade so that the profits would go into the royal treasury.

The wars and revolutions of the eighteenth century, both in Europe and the Americas, had a great effect on Cuba. In 1762, during the Seven Years' War between the European nations, the British occupied Havana. During this ten-month takeover, trade between Cuba and the British colonies in the New World was established. After regaining control of Cuba, the Spanish crown tried to keep the profitable colony content by allowing it to trade with other countries.

The French Revolution of 1789 also contributed to the transformation of Cuba from a minor shipping outpost to an enormously prosperous colony. Revolution in France inspired slave revolts in the French colony of Haiti. Under the leadership of a former slave, François Dominique Toussaint L'Ouverture, the rebels succeeded in a violent takeover of Haiti. White planters were killed or expelled from the new black republic. Over 30,000 French refugees settled in Cuba and brought their knowledge and culture with them.

Cuba soon replaced Haiti as the major cultivator of sugar. When there weren't enough natives to do the work needed, the planters brought in slaves from Africa. As the plantation owners prospered, the slave population grew.

Slavery conditions were somewhat different in Cuba than the United States. In Cuba, slaves were allowed to own and sell property and could buy their family's freedom. Also, the child of a slave and a colonist was born free. Laborers from China were brought in to replace the slaves.

Slavery in Cuba was no less cruelly inhuman than it was elsewhere. Taken from their African homes and families and imprisoned on slave ships, up to half the captives died from illness, punishment, or suicide before they reached Cuba. Bought and sold by the white settlers and housed in **bohíos** (huts) or **barracoons** (dormitories), the slaves were forced to toil for long hours in the fields under threat of physical punishment. Even so, the slaves repeatedly rebelled. Slavery did not end in Cuba, however, until almost the end of the nineteenth century.

The nineteenth century brought revolution to Spain's colonies in South America. One by one, the colonies gained their independence. In Cuba, the **criollos**, Cuban-born whites, dreamed of shaking the domination of Spain and the **peninsulares**, Spanish-born whites.

On October 10, 1868, rebellious **criollo** planters at Yara, in easternmost Oriente province, declared their independence from Spain in the "Grito de Yara" proclamation. Led by Carlos Manuel de Céspedes, the planters freed their slaves, who joined them in the fighting. The rebels, or **mambisos,** gained control of about half the island in the course of their guerrilla warfare in the Sierra Maestra mountains. This Ten Years' War, as it came to be known, ended in 1878 with a promise of reforms, including the abolition of slavery, which did not come about, however, until 1886. The struggle for independence continued, its supporters inspired by the ideals of Cuba's great poet and hero, José Martí, "Apostle of Freedom."

Born in Havana on January 28, 1853, José Martí was a promising student from a poor family. When still a boy, he was introduced to democratic ideas and developed strong feelings against slavery and the oppressive Spanish-controlled government. At seventeen, the idealistic Martí was arrested for writing a letter condemning a classmate's participation in a pro-Spanish demonstration. For this he was sentenced to six years in prison. After months spent breaking rocks on a chain gang and enduring harsh jail conditions, Martí was deported to Spain in 1871. During his exile he studied law. He also began a career in writing which brought him worldwide renown. Through his poetry, plays, children's stories, and articles in newspapers and magazines, Martí communicated his political beliefs.

From 1880 to 1895 José Martí lived in New York City. Tirelessly, he made speeches, taught classes, raised funds and sought support for his cause. Martí planned a revolution which would bring an end to Spanish control of his homeland, improve the conditions of the poor people, and end the inequalities between black and white. He organized the **Partido Revolucionario Cubano** (Cuban Revolutionary Party) in New York in 1892. Along with the veteran

Jose Martí.

black commander of the Ten Years War, Antonio Maceo, Martí made plans for an invasion of Cuba.

On February 24, 1895, rebel military forces led by Maceo and Máximo Gómez attacked Cuba. In April, Martí joined the fighting, and on May 19, 1895, he was killed in battle. Jose Martí still symbolizes an heroic ideal to Cubans and other Latin Americans.

Martí's death did not end the war. The toll of death and destruction grew. In the United States, public opinion was turned against Spain by newspaper reports of atrocities against the rebels. The U.S. battleship 'Maine' was sent to Havana to protect American citizens there. On February 15, 1898, the ship mysteriously exploded and sank, killing

The U.S.S. 'Maine.'

266 crew members. Blaming Spain, the United States demanded she get out of Cuba. Certain politicians and newspapers inflamed public sentiment for war, and Spain, against her will, declared war on the U.S. In turn, the United States Congress declared war on Spain retroactively. United States forces, including Theodore Roosevelt's Rough Riders, invaded Cuba. "Remember the 'Maine' " was the battle cry of the Spanish-American War. Six months after it began, the fighting was over, and 400 years of Spanish empire ended.

The Treaty of Paris, which ended the war, established Cuba as an independent republic. But the United States remained in military occupation until 1902. During the occupation, United States doctors wiped out yellow fever and a public school system for Cuban children was set up. The United States, however, did not allow Cuba's independence until certain conditions, known as the Platt Amendment, were added to the new Cuban constitution. These conditions included giving the United States the right to lease land for a naval base on Cuban territory and to intervene militarily should events on the island seem to affect the U.S. Upon the Cubans' reluctant acceptance of the Platt Amendment, Tomás Estrada Palma became the first elected president of the Cuban Republic on May 20, 1902 — Cuba's Independence Day. Continuing political unrest in Cuba led to U.S. military intervention from 1906 to 1909 and again in 1912.

Cuba joined the Allies in World War I. Great increases in United States investments and trade in Cuba soon made

An aerial view of part of the U.S. Naval Base at Guantanamo Bay.

the new nation economically dependent upon its northern neighbor and also made Cuba very prosperous. After the war, however, a drop in sugar prices caused an economic crisis which brought about unrest among the people who were desperate for work and money. To control the country, Gerardo Machado, who was elected president in 1924, assumed the powers of a dictator. But Machado's regime provoked violent opposition, especially among university students. On September 4, 1933, an army revolt organized by Sergeant Fulgencio Batista y Zaldivar was successful. Batista ruled Cuba through a series of puppet presidents at first. Then Batista was himself elected in 1940. Under Batista, a treaty was signed with the United States ending the Platt Amendment. However, the U.S. was allowed to continue to lease the land for the Guantanamo Bay Naval Base. Favorable trade relations with the United States continued. By this time, United States investors controlled

Fulgencio Batista.

75% of the sugar crop as well as most of the tobacco, mining, and cattle-raising interests, and the public utilities.

Batista retired after his term as president expired. But just before the election of 1952, Batista led a **coup d'état**, a plot to overthrow the government. Successful, Batista this time set himself up as dictator.

Throughout Batista's rule, Cuba's industries continued to bring large profits to U.S. and Cuban investors. Tourists from the United States flocked to Cuba's luxurious resort areas, and tourism was one of the country's most important resources. A large middle class of prosperous Cubans flourished, but thousands of poor people lived in slums.

Fidel Castro during the revolution. The bearded soldier is Camillo Cienfuegos who, after becoming an important part of the government, was to disappear under mysterious circumstances. The other soldier is Raul Castro.

Children and adults begged on the streets. In the country, few children over 12 attended school. Except for the four-month sugar harvest, as many as 700,000 people were unemployed. Racial discrimination barred blacks and mulattoes from beaches, restaurants, and skilled jobs.

Opposition to Batista corruption grew among all classes of Cubans. The protests were led by university students, among them a young lawyer, Dr. Fidel Castro Ruz. Born on August 13, 1926 in Oriente province, Castro became involved in political protests as a young student. After Batista's 1952 coup, Castro went to court to try to have the dictatorial government declared illegal but he failed. Castro turned to armed rebellion. He organized an attack on the Moncada army barracks in Santiago de Cuba. The attack was put down and captured rebels were tortured and killed. Castro himself was imprisoned.

Ernesto "Che" Guevara.

After his release from prison, Castro went to Mexico, where he organized and trained a group of exiles for a revolutionary invasion of Cuba. Numbering only eighty-two men, the group sailed to Cuba in a small yacht, the **Granma**. On landing in Oriente, they were met by Batista's forces. Only twelve revolutionaries survived the battle and they retreated into the wild Sierra Maestra mountains. These few men—among them Castro, his brother Raul, and a young Argentinian doctor named Ernesto "Che" Guevara —started a guerrilla war which soon attracted many more rebels. They moved swiftly, striking out against Batista's army in surprise attacks and then disappearing into the wilderness. The rebels rarely slept in the same place more than one night. They fought with captured weapons and often went without food. They let their hair and beards grow long. The "Beards," as they were often called, made friends with the peasants by paying well for supplies and listening to their grievances. Between battles, Che treated sick people who had never seen a doctor.

Like José Martí, Castro promised sweeping changes including free elections, an honest government, land, schools, jobs and health care for all, and an end to United States economic domination. Castro became a kind of Robin Hood to the Cubans. Many flocked to his banner— students, politicians, city workers, the middle class, and the army.

Faced with rebellion all about him, Batista fled the country, and the revolutionary forces led by Fidel Castro marched into Havana on the eighth of January, 1959.

New Cuba and the World

As the whole world watched, the bearded Castro declared himself Prime Minister of Cuba. He and his army set into motion their promised programs for reform. Rents were lowered, racial discrimination forbidden. All estates and farms larger than a thousand acres were taken from their owners and **nationalized,** made the property of the government. Most of the seized land, including over 2¼ million acres once owned by United States investors, was turned into large state-owned farms. Some payment was offered to the owners, but most of them, increasingly fearful, fled the country. Many of Batista's supporters were

Fidel Castro making a speech. Attendance is usually compulsory.

arrested, and so were many who were suspected of any antagonism to Castro. Property left behind by the exiles or those imprisoned was taken over by the government. Castro nationalized the telephone company, sugar mills, and electric utilities.

The total worth of seized U.S. property was estimated at 2 billion dollars. The United States stopped buying Cuban sugar to protest seizures of its citizens' property. Then the U.S. broke off diplomatic relations in January 1961.

Meanwhile, Cuban exiles in the States who wanted to return to their homeland were secretly training for an invasion of Cuba. They had the assistance of President John F. Kennedy and the U.S. government. The invasion took place on April 17, 1961, at the Bay of Pigs, **Playa Girón**. The invaders were defeated within seventy-two hours. Over 1200

Commemorating Soviet-Cuban friendship.

men were captured and held captive until the U.S. government paid $50 million in food and medical supplies to ransom them.

Castro turned to the Soviet Union, which had already offered to buy Cuba's sugar and pay for it with weapons. The Soviet Union installed secret bases on Cuba from which missiles could attack the United States. In October 1962 President Kennedy ordered a naval blockade of the island. After days of tense negotiations, with the whole world anxiously watching, the Soviet Union withdrew the missiles.

Cuba had been one of the original members of the Organization of American States (OAS) created in 1948. The OAS was set up to work with the United Nations to promote the welfare of the western hemisphere. But when

Cuba publicized her intentions to spread revolution by guerrilla warfare to other Latin-American countries, she was expelled from the Organization. Cuba was isolated from the rest of Latin America by a trade embargo. This led to many shortages and economic problems.

Again the Soviet Union came to Castro's assistance. The Soviets provided military aid, scientific and technical assistance, loans, trade privileges, and political support. The Soviets became Cuba's closest ally.

Castro encouraged revolutionary movements in other Latin American countries, angering their governments. But after Che Guevara died fighting with Bolivian rebels in 1967, Castro's support of guerrilla activities lessened. Relations with Latin America improved, and over the years Cuba gained the respect of the world's developing nations for its social progress.

Although Cuba was no longer a member of the OAS after 1962, it continued to participate in the activities of the United Nations, of which it was a founding member. Castro spoke before the U.N. General Assembly in New York in 1960 and again in 1979.

However, relations between Cuba and the United States reflected continued hostility and resentment on both sides. Castro demanded that the U.S. end the trade embargo and give up its naval base at Guantanamo. In the United States, the Cuban exile community publicized reports of human rights violations by the Castro government. Nor had Cuba compensated United States companies for properties that had been seized.

Visits to Cuba by individual members of Congress trying to improve relations during the mid-1970s helped ease the tension between the two countries. The door was opened for cultural and sports exchanges. President Jimmy Carter authorized negotiations on maritime matters and eased travel restrictions in 1977.

Cuban-United States relations deteriorated again when Castro sent 15,000 advisers and soldiers to fight on the side of Soviet-backed rebel movements in Africa. The United States objected to Cuba's military intervention in Angola and Ethiopia and to the reported presence of Cuban military advisers in more than 15 African nations.

Then in April 1980, about 11,000 discontented Cuban citizens demanded political asylum at the Peruvian embassy in Havana. Castro declared the port of Mariel open to anyone desiring to leave, at the same time taking the opportunity to unload Cuban undesirables. Cuban-Americans

Cuban refugees, 1980 — **Marielos** — arrive in a dangerously overcrowded boat, and are intercepted by the U.S. Coast Guard.

Coast Guard medical technician from the cutter "Dallas" tends to one of the passengers on the boat.

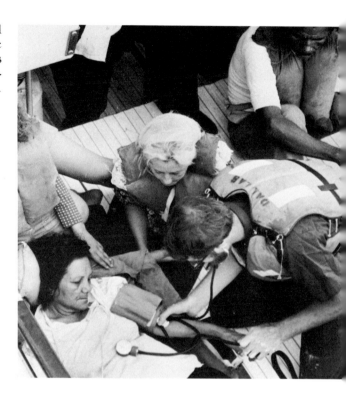

These **Marielos** are waiting for U.S. Immigration officials to find them a place in the States.

came from Florida in a flotilla of small boats to pick up relatives and friends. At Mariel they found that for every relative or friend they took out, they also had to bring over six undesirables. The U.S. government was in a dilemma: deny access to the United States to everyone, or take the bad with the good. For humane reasons, President Carter chose the latter course.

In all, between April and September, over 125,000 Cubans entered the United States. In Cuba, millions of demonstrators shouted, "Good riddance to the criminals!" as Castro emptied out Cuban jails and mental hospitals. For the average citizens who fled to the United States to join their families or to try to achieve higher economic status, the transition to the free enterprise system may be difficult, because they have grown up in a different kind of society.

People's Power

Fidel Castro, using his power as leader of the revolution, controlled the government of Cuba without elections for 18 years. Although he promised democratic elections in his revolutionary program, he governed as dictator. Then in February 1976, Cuban voters went to the polls. A constitution was approved and a government called **Poder Popular,** "People's Power," was formed. According to the new constitution, Cuba is a socialist state. All of Cuba's land, natural resources, industries, enterprises, and buildings are under state control.

Over 4.8 million Cubans over age 14 belong to Committees for the Defense of the Revolution (CDR). CDR members protect their neighborhoods and keep track of the inhabitants' health and welfare—and their activities. Members also meet to discuss local events and political affairs. CDRs pick candidates from among their members for election to Provincial and Municipal Assemblies of People's Power. There are 14 Provincial and 169 Municipal Assemblies, one for each province and municipality. The voting age is 16.

The National Assembly of People's Power is the nation's legislative body. The Communist Party of Cuba **(Partido Comunista Cubano)** is the only political party permitted, but not all delegates to the National Assembly are members of the Party. All delegates are elected at one time, and serve a five-year term. The Assembly meets at least twice a year to pass laws and approve budgets, treaties, and appointments of state ministers. The Assembly also supervises all other government organizations, and it has the sole power to declare war. At their first meeting, the delegates elect a thirty-member Council of State which governs when the National Assembly is not in session.

The first National Assembly of People's Power in 1976 elected Fidel Castro as president of the Council of State. According to Cuban law, Castro is therefore head of state and head of government. He is also president of the Council of Ministers, the executive branch of government which makes policies to be carried out by the administrative departments or ministries, and supreme commander of the

armed forces. In addition, Castro heads the Communist Party of Cuba, which the constitution declares is the "leading force of society and the state." The top government and Communist Party officials are **fidelistas** or "loyal followers of Fidel." Raul Castro, the President's brother, is second in command.

Thus, although a new government structure with a constitutional base has been established, Fidel Castro is still all-powerful and a very personal leader. Fidel, as all Cubans call him, is a familiar figure to workers, schoolchildren, and people on the street. Cubans who spot him driving his jeep through their neighborhoods, dressed in his usual green army uniform, may stop him to ask questions or invite him to join in a baseball game.

The Cuban constitution guarantees medical care, food, clothing, housing, education, and work to all citizens. All Cubans are considered under the constitution to be equal, and discrimination on the basis of race, sex, color, or national origin is prohibited. Technically, freedoms of speech, religion, assembly, and press are allowed, but these are restricted. These freedoms cannot be exercised in opposition to the goals of the government. Nor can individuals leave the country without special permission. The government is considered more important than the individual. Individuals do have the right to their personal property, savings, small landholdings, and profits from the sales or produce from their gardens.

Ordinary citizens act as judges in Cuba's courts, serving without pay. The worker judges preside over informal trials held in local meeting places after working hours. More difficult cases or those which may result in prison sentences are sent to higher courts which have professional judges as well as worker judges. There are no juries. All lawyers work

A people's court.

for the government, and every citizen is entitled to legal defense.

In general, Cuba's crime rate is low. Punishment is stern. And because boys join the army at sixteen, the number of youthful offenders has dropped. However, the Cuban government has designated new forms of crime: loafing, unexcused absence from work, selling on the black market, and destruction of government property. These are considered serious crimes punishable by imprisonment.

Most Cuban prisons are work farms where inmates work and attend classes to learn new skills. Persons convicted of sabotage and other counterrevolutionary crimes are held in maximum security prisons. The number of Cubans in jail for crimes of political belief and antigovernment activities is in dispute. In 1976, Fidel Castro told television personality Barbara Walters that there were about 3000 political prisoners. Cuban exile groups in the United States report ten times that number.

The Revolutionary Armed Forces of Cuba (**Fuerzas Armadas Revolucionarias,** FAR) is one of the three largest military forces in Latin America. The latest weapons and military equipment are supplied by the Soviet Union. The Soviets also opened their space program to Cuba. The first Cuban astronaut, Arnaldo Tamayo Mendez, went into space on a Soviet spaceship in 1980.

Military service is compulsory for boys. All sixteen-year-old boys must enlist for three years. After basic training, many are made part of the Youth Labor Army which works on agricultural and construction projects around the island. Boys and girls wanting to make a career of the military attend special military high schools from which future officers are selected. Even elementary school-children receive military training, including practice in handling and shooting rifles. The Cuban slogan is **"Patria o muerte"** — "Homeland or death!"

Agriculture
and
Industry

Cuba is a socialist republic, but sugar is still king. For over two hundred years, the island's economy has been based on this major crop and Cuba is one of the world's three largest sugar producers.

Today, more and more of the work—plowing, planting, fertilizing, and harvesting—on the state-owned sugar plantations is done by machine. However, at harvest time large numbers of workers move into the cane fields with machetes to cut the cane. When the cane is ripe it must be cut down and gathered quickly so that it reaches the mills while the sugar content is at its highest. The cane is transported by truck and railroad to mills where the sweet juice is pressed out and then boiled down by machines into crude sugar. The crude sugar, which is gray in color, is sold abroad. For Cuban consumption, crude sugar is processed into white sugar at refineries. By-products of sugar processing include molasses, sugar juice used in making rum and other beverages, and crushed cane stalks or **bagasse**. **Bagasse** is used widely for fuel, pulp and paper, and animal feed.

"Let us make a more efficient and productive sugar harvest."

Machetero cutting sugar cane with his machete.

The government tried to end Cuba's dependence on sugar exports by building industries to make the things that would otherwise have to be imported. It was unsuccessful and sugar is still Cuba's most important industry, because sugar buys the other products Cuba needs. The income from sugar sales is used to purchase industrial equipment, fuel oil, raw materials, and food. Dependence on sugar means that the rise and fall of sugar prices seriously affect the nation's economy. At times the price has risen to 65¢ a pound or fallen to 7¢. The Soviet Union buys Cuban sugar at a constant price, about 30¢ a pound, to help its ally keep economically stable when sugar prices are low.

After losing the United States as a trading partner, Cuba developed markets for its agricultural exports in Europe, Canada, and Latin America. For example, grapefruit cultivated by high school students on the Isle of Youth are a leading new export to Canada.

Crops grown in Cuba today include rice, citrus fruit, corn, potatoes, tomatoes, bananas, and cotton. Improved methods for livestock and poultry raising have resulted in more meat, milk, and eggs in the average Cuban's diet.

Cuban cowboys bring the cows in for milking.

Cuba's fishing industry has grown from solitary fishermen in their own small wooden boats to seven fleets of modern vessels owned by the state. Much of the catch is exported to the Soviet Union and European nations.

A central planning group runs most enterprises from the largest sugar plantations to the smallest neighborhood shops. All that remains in private hands is small farms — under 165 acres in size — on which most of Cuba's tobacco

Although this farmhouse has a thatched roof, it also has electrical wiring and a carport.

and coffee are raised. These crops require the specialized care possible on a small farm.

Coffee bushes grow on hills and mountainsides. The coffee beans must be picked by hand as they ripen and then turned frequently as they cure or dry in the sun. The leaves of several kinds of tobacco plants, some planted in sunlight and some in shade, are also picked and cured by hand. The various colored leaves are sorted and sent to government-owned cigarette and cigar factories. Today, as in the past, expert factory workers, particularly in Havana, deftly roll

This farmhouse has a well (center) to supply the occupants.

the finest leaves into cigars, while listening to someone read the latest news, poetry, and political messages.

Cuba has enormous reserves of nickel, iron, chrome, cobalt, and copper. However, extracting and purifying them has been a difficult problem.

Industry is growing in Cuba. The oldest and largest industry is food processing. Nonfood items produced in Cuban factories include textiles, ships, cement, tires, shoes, fertilizers, medicines, sports equipment, and machinery. Small workshops make musical instruments, needlecrafts, and woodwork. Tourism is also growing once again. Old hotels have been renovated and new ones built.

Castro's message is, "The most sacred duty of this generation of workers is to consecrate itself to the development of the country, to think more of development than of consumption."

Some citizens complain that products made in Cuba are sold to other countries and are not available in their neighborhood stores. The economic planners explain that Cuba needs to export its products in order to obtain items it cannot produce, like heavy machinery, chemicals, buses, trucks, and petroleum. Cubans must do without.

Although some economic recovery has been made, Cuba is still a poor and underdeveloped country. The economy depends on agriculture, and can be badly hurt if natural disasters like hurricanes, drought, plant pests or diseases harm the crops.

Cubans are eager to buy United States goods in exchange for sugar, seafood, tropical fruit, and cigars. They look forward to a future reopening of trade with the United States.

Cuba
at
Work

Cuba is a nation of workers. Every man and woman has the right to a job and to a salary paid by the government. Often, however, the jobs are not of their own choosing. People can also be made to change jobs. According to the new constitution, work is now a "right and duty and a source of pride for every citizen." Even elementary school-children are taught to respect the value of labor — they raise vegetables. High school students devote half the school day to work in factories or on farms attached to their schools. College students, city workers, housewives, and

Returning to school after a morning of farm work.

military recruits volunteer to work on farms and building sites. The Latin American Stadium in Havana was built by 300,000 Cuban volunteers. However, those who are unable to work are given food, clothing, housing, and medical care.

After Castro's revolution, most of the country's middle class professionals and technicians left the country. Those who stayed had to learn how to run the factories, plantations, schools, and hospitals. The new managers faced difficulties and failures at first. But given the opportunity to study, and to learn on the job, the workers gained experience and confidence.

Cubans work forty hours a week and take one month vacation every year. Free day care is provided for children as young as one and one-half months while their parents

The blackboard in this bakery is used to keep track of production quotas and the daily consumption of flour, shortening, and eggs.

work. All workers, whether doctor, barber, plant manager, or restaurant waiter, are paid by the state, which also keeps any profits. Wages depend on the skills and output of the worker. A skilled technician in a factory may make more than the supervisor. Since health care, education, and

Operating a printing press.

recreation activities are free, and housing and food inexpensive (unless the food is bought on the black market), Cuban workers can save a little money. However, the government provides other incentives than money for good workers. Some receive medals or special commendations. Others may be awarded tickets to a cultural event or a free vacation trip. Scarce items, such as refrigerators, televisions, or new apartments, are sometimes given to the most productive and enthusiastic workers. The winners are chosen by their fellow workers.

Cubans usually live close to their jobs. All over the island, new towns have been built around factories and

A butcher shop in Trinidad.

state farms. After a day's work, men and women may
return from their homes to the workplace to attend classes
at the workers' school. Workers meet together to plan im-
provements and new goals for their industries. They also
discuss politics and recommend fellow workers for further
education and training and for Communist Party member-

ship. Some groups may take time off to build housing while co-workers take over their tasks temporarily.

President Fidel Castro has frequently pointed out that all labor is service to the state. People who are unemployed or absent from their jobs without reason may be taken to court. Everyone is asked to make sacrifices so that Castro's economic plans will be fulfilled.

The milkman comes on horseback in Trinidad.

Sports,
The Arts,
and Recreation

Cuba's recent achievements in international sports competitions are the source of great national pride. In August 1980, a team of Cuban athletes was given a joyous welcome home from the Moscow Olympics. Among the twenty medal winners was Téofilo Stevenson, three-time Olympic heavyweight boxing champion and javelin thrower María Caridad Colón, the first Latin American woman ever to win an Olympic gold medal. Since 1960, Cuban athletes

The sports stadium in Havana.

have brought home forty-six Olympic medals. At the Pan-American Games in 1971, 1975, and 1979, Cuba came in second only to the United States.

At home, too, sports events are enormously popular and are encouraged and supported by the government. At the many sports arenas, admission is free.

Baseball is Cuba's national pastime. Before the revolution, many Cuban players were picked to play on major league teams in the United States. Cuban-American baseball stars include Bert Campaneris, Tony Perez, and Luis Tiant.

In high school and college, President Fidel Castro was a superior athlete who thought of becoming a professional pitcher. Through Castro's influence, Cubans now are avid participants in sports for exercise, recreation, and entertainment. They join in school, workplace, and neighborhood sports organizations.

All Cuban athletes are amateurs who practice and play in their nonworking hours. Team members are given time off to compete in international events, as did the amateur baseball team that won the World Baseball Championship for the sixteenth time in 1980. Other popular sports include soccer, basketball, boxing, volleyball, track-and-field, swimming, and gymnastics. The most popular nonathletic pastimes are chess and dominoes.

Although Cubans work hard, they are also a fun-loving people. Children have a good time riding their bicycles or playing stickball after school. Everyone enjoys visiting

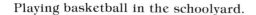
Playing basketball in the schoolyard.

There is no school on Saturday afternoons.

friends or relatives and strolling to the town plaza in the evening. On hot summer days, surf and sand lure young and old to the beaches.

July is carnival time in Cuba, when the end of the year's sugar harvest (**zafra**), and the 26th of July holiday (the anniversary of Castro's attack on Batista's barracks), are celebrated. Families travel to Havana and Santiago de Cuba, where the biggest festivals take place. Over several days and nights, thousands of people join in lively parades of costumed dancers and musicians while others enjoy just

watching the entertainment and fireworks. The end of **zafra** also signals the beginning of vacation for most workers and students. The resorts are filled with Cuban families enjoying a month-long holiday at the beach, mountains, or in the national parks.

Today, through television, radio, books, films, and traveling performance groups, the arts reach even the most remote areas of the country. Cuba's culture is rich with the influences of its varied ethnic heritage. Classical music and literature of the Spanish mix with rhythms and rituals of

Carnival time.

A small book bindery.

the African. Popular and symphonic music, ballet, and films from the United States, western Europe, and the Soviet Union, all belong to Cuban culture. At the arts school at Cubanacan, built on former President Batista's golf course, young people selected for their talent study music, art, and dance.

Since the early 1800s, poetry has been the major form of literary expression in Cuba. The poems of José Martí, through which he expressed his social and ethical beliefs, inspired generations of Cubans and won worldwide recognition. Among twentieth century poets, Nicolás Guillén is respected for combining Afro-Cuban rhythms with Spanish lyrics to portray the lives of poor Cuban blacks and mulattoes. Alejo Carpentier was a noted novelist and scholar. Young writers today give expression to conflicts within the revolutionary society through poetry, short stories, and novels. Writers are free to criticize the shortcomings and mistakes of Cuban society—but not the system itself.

Cubans love movies and the government has brought this form of entertainment to people even in remote mountain areas by truck and mule. Cuban and United States films are very popular and they can be seen at movie theaters or on television. The nation's many government-run television and radio stations emphasize educational and news programs, but also broadcast sports and entertain-

Singer and orchestra at a local dance.

ment shows. Cuban radios and televisions can pick up broadcasts from Florida. Cuba's national and provincial newspapers are all published by government organizations which determine their contents.

The works of Cuban artists are on display in museums and galleries. Wilfredo Lam is a world-famous painter, of Chinese and black ancestry. His paintings reflect Afro-Cuban culture as well as the influence of European art. Afro-Cuban themes are also seen in the sculptural works of Teodoro Ramos Blanco. Few limits were placed on artists after the revolution. The works of young artists are often experimental in form. Murals, posters, and photographs are created by artists and designers for the purpose of informing, educating, and entertaining the public.

The director of the National Ballet of Cuba is Alicia Alonso, a ballerina admired all over the world for her artistry, particularly because of her long struggle against blindness. Young students are selected from across the country to train for careers as dancers at the National Ballet School. Other companies perform modern and folkloric dance forms throughout city and countryside, and abroad. Theater groups based in urban and rural areas perform the works of new playwrights.

Cuban music has long been famous for its blend of Spanish and African rhythms. The early Ciboney Indians played drums and **maracas** made from the fruit of the wild calabash tree. Bongo drums are Cuban in origin. From the folk music tradition came the **rumba, mambo, conga, chacha** and **son** universally familiar. Ernesto Lecuona wrote many popular songs which became international hits.

TV reaches into even remote rural homes.

Cuba's outstanding classical composers, Amadeo Roldán and Alejandro Caturla both wrote music in pre-Castro times inspired by Afro-Cuban traditions. Classical and popular music are enjoyed all over the island due to the increasing number of orchestras and musical groups, the growing recording industry, and radio and television programs.

Social Progress

Cuba led Latin America in literacy, but even so, in 1959 about one-fourth of the population of Cuba could not read or write. One of the first projects of the new government was a year-long campaign during which 270,000 volunteers went into poor rural and urban areas as teachers to improve the level of literacy.

Today not only children but also parents and grandparents attend school. The aim is to achieve at least a sixth grade education for all Cubans. Each year, over 400,000

"On my honor I pledge to achieve the sixth grade."

Young women learn pattern making.

A new apartment building.

adults are encouraged to sign up for free after-work classes. Some study for high school, technical, and university degrees.

Cuban homes are designed to attract cool breezes. Windows have wooden shutters to keep out the sun during the day. Most homes have porches or balconies because

Cubans enjoy sitting outside in the evening. No home is without a rocking chair, its seat and back made of cane to allow cool air to reach its occupant.

Providing housing for all has been a difficult challenge for the government. Slum buildings were torn down, their former occupants moved into free or inexpensive apartments in the confiscated homes of Cubans who fled the country. In rural areas, many peasant families moved into new apartments on state-owned farms. The huts where others still live have been improved with conveniences like electricity and indoor plumbing.

The countryside.

Inside a Cuban home — welcomed with a smile.

In new apartments, the kitchen is too small to eat in — it is for working only. Not every family has a refrigerator, so marketing must be done often. However, most homes have a television as well as a radio. On the walls hang family photographs and pictures of Castro or Che Guevara. Some Cubans display religious pictures or shrines.

Often large families must share a small apartment. It is especially difficult for newly-married couples to find a new house. A request to move must be approved by the government. Waiting lists are long.

Cubans are very proud of their excellent health care system. In 1959 Castro's government took over hospitals and clinics and offered free medical care. However, almost half of the island's 6300 doctors left the country with many other medical professionals and technicians, creating an acute shortage of medical workers. An emergency training program was started. At the same time, local members of the Committees for the Defense of the Revolution joined in a nationwide campaign to prevent disease by improving sanitary conditions. And every child and adult was inoculated against diphtheria, polio, and other diseases.

The newly-trained doctors and nurses set up hospitals and clinics in the countryside. Today, the medical and dental care in remote areas is equal to Havana's. And over 1500 Cuban doctors have gone abroad, helping African, Asian, and other Latin American nations improve health care conditions.

Scene at a countryside clinic.

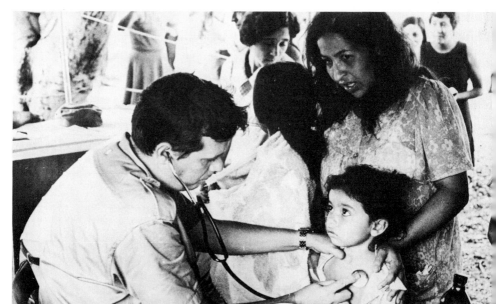

Foreign medical experts agree that Cuba is now the healthiest country in Latin America. Life expectancy today is seventy years compared to forty-eight years in Bolivia and the infant death figure is at 19.3 per thousand births compared to 94.3 per thousand in Paraguay. Almost all serious infectious and parasitic diseases have been eliminated in Cuba.

Cuba's treatment of mental patients is also a model for other developing nations. Havana Psychiatric Hospital patients work at gardening, preparing food, cleaning, making

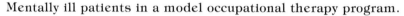

Mentally ill patients in a model occupational therapy program.

uniforms and furniture, and entertaining other patients with amusements like orchestral concerts. They are paid for their work and can send money home to their families. Patients can leave when doctors consider them well enough to cope with normal life.

Cuba's free social service system extends from birth to retirement and old age. Health care, education, and housing are provided for every citizen. But Cuba is still a poor country. The basic needs of the people are met, but there are few luxuries.

When a Cuban goes shopping, he or she must bring the family ration book along with the grocery money. The ration tickets determine how many eggs or how much rice can be bought. In Cuba, food items and consumer products that are in short supply are rationed so that everyone will have

Shopping center.

an equal share. For example, each person may buy only one pair of shoes a year. If greater quantities of an item are available, the government will sell them without ration tickets. Because all legal stores are run by the government, there is no competition between different brands, nor are there any advertisements. Some Cubans buy additional goods on the illegal black market. These black marketeers risk arrest and punishment.

There is usually a line at the grocery store.

Eating out in restaurants is very popular; no ration tickets are necessary. People wait in line for their favorite flavor of **Coppelia** ice cream. There are only two kinds of sodas; **la rubia** (blond) is like ginger ale, and **la prieta** (dark) is like cola.

Favorite foods still include black beans with rice, chicken or pork with rice, fried plantains (a kind of banana), and roast pork. However, the eating habits of the Cuban

Music is relaxing after work.

people have been changed by the availability of new varieties of food. In the past, poor Cubans rarely ate fish, eggs, or green vegetables. By making these products cheap and readily available, the government has encouraged a more balanced and nutritious diet.

Some traditions are more difficult to change. Until the 1950s, many Cuban girls were raised in the strict old-fashioned Spanish belief that women should not work outside the home. Women who needed to earn money were thought to be suited only to domestic work. Unmarried young women were not allowed to go out alone. Married women were supposed to serve their families and obey their husbands. Today, these beliefs have been changed in Cuba as in the rest of the world.

Most Cuban women hold outside jobs. The government encourages women to work by providing day care for children. Many offices open later in the day so that women workers can go shopping before work. New Cuban law requires that both husband and wife share household tasks and child-raising responsibilities.

There is still some sex discrimination in Cuba as in other countries. The Federation of Cuban Women represents the interests of women and works to end sex discrimination. The Federation is headed by Vilma Espin, who fought alongside Fidel Castro in the revolution.

Religious faith is not encouraged in Cuba today. Since Spanish colonial days, most Cubans have been Roman Catholics although there are also Protestant and Jewish congregations. The only distinctly Cuban religion is

The Havana Cathedral.

Santeria, a black religious sect with a basis in witchcraft. **Santeria** has many followers among descendants of Nigerian Yoruba people. They believe that Yoruba spirits and Catholic saints are the same powerful forces. **Santeria** services combine drumming and singing in the Yoruba language with Roman Catholic rituals.

After Castro declared that his goal was a Communist society, many church leaders were indirectly forced to leave. Church lands were seized by the government and the clergy feared religious persecution. Today, the churches are open for services, although attended mostly by the elderly.

Contemporary Cuba has been especially successful in eliminating racial discrimination, inherited from the days of slavery. The new government declared that all Cubans, black and white, are **mestizos** in spirit. Today, all jobs are integrated, as are housing, restaurants, hotels, and schools. Any remaining prejudices are severely criticized.

Children
Today

There is a slogan in Cuba today, often repeated on billboards and posters, which declares "there is nothing more important than a child." Cuba's future is closely tied to the lives of children—over half of the population was born since the 1959 revolution. Children are the only privileged group in the new society.

The National Assembly of People's Power adopted a Code on Children and Youth in 1978 which describes the legal rights and also the responsibilities of young people.

"Nothing is more important than a child."

Among the obligations of children stated in this law is dedication to study and work.

Education is free. Preschool education begins at age two, and children must attend school until they are fourteen. The government hopes one day to extend compulsory education through high school.

From the seventh to tenth grades, many students from city and farm leave their homes to live, study, and work together. Each new high school consists of a group of con-

A technical high school outside Havana.

crete buildings built around a central plaza. The complex, built for 500 boys and girls, includes dormitories, classrooms, a dining hall, movie theater, sports area, assembly hall, medical center, and a student store. Attached to the school is a large farm or fruit orchard of over a thousand acres.

All high school students receive free tuition, room and board, uniforms, books, and traveling expenses. On school days, the students arise at 6 A.M. After a breakfast of buttered bread and coffee with milk, half the students go to

Secondary school in the countryside.

A math class smiles at the camera.

their classes, and the rest go to work on the farm. At the lunch break, the two groups switch activities. In the seventh grade the required subjects include mathematics, physics, biology, geography, history, Spanish, English, technical training, and physical education. In this work-study program, the hours spent in the fields are as important as classroom time. The crops produced by the students help pay for the school's expenses.

In addition to physical work and study, each day's schedule includes sports, cultural activities, one half hour of free time, then more study until the lights go out at

10 P.M. After early morning classes on Saturday, the students are taken by bus to their homes. They return to school at 10 P.M. the next day. Boys and girls are responsible for keeping school and living areas clean. When they can, parents visit their children at school and join in cleanups and farmwork.

Some high schools concentrate on technical skills. At the Lenin Vocational School in Havana, students assemble radios, televisions, and electronic components which are sold throughout the country. Each year the best students win a trip to the Soviet Union.

There are also special high schools for teacher training. These students act as instructors in nearby elementary schools even before they graduate.

Cuban students must pass examinations to be promoted. The students with the best grades in the tenth grade graduating class are selected to go on to higher education, if their political convictions conform to the Communist way of thinking. Some attend advanced programs in agriculture or industry. Others are chosen to prepare for jobs as high school teachers, translators, musicians, artists, or public health workers.

The brightest students are chosen to prepare for university studies. At Cuba's four universities, students study for degrees in medicine, engineering, architecture, science, economics, humanities, agriculture, and teaching. The need for specialists in certain fields rather than free choice determines a student's course of study.

Two Pioneers.

Most young people belong to the Pioneers, a politically inspired group which organizes recreational activities after school and during vacations. Pioneers aged seven to four-teen participate in community service and sports and learn music, art, and dance. They also receive political, vocational, and military training with the objective of becoming future Communist Party members. Pioneers wear red berets and blue and white scarves with their school uniforms. They have their own weekly newspaper. In 1979, a huge Pioneer Palace was completed near Havana for the use and benefit of the children—something like YMCAs and YWCAs.

Only twenty-five years ago, visitors to Cuba saw children begging on the street, barefoot and suffering from hunger and disease. Today no Cuban child goes hungry or without adequate clothing. Every child gets a free education. Their activities are regimented, and freedom of choice is limited, but no one is deprived.

At the official opening of the Pioneer Palace in 1979, President Fidel Castro said:

"This year we're celebrating the International Year of the Child, like all countries of the world. However, for us, for our Socialist Revolution, every year is Year of the Child. Every month, every day, every hour, every minute is the month, day, hour, and minute of the child. What has the Revolution been dedicated to for the last twenty years if not to this?"

Index

94